NEW AND SELECTED POEMS

Henri Coulette (1927–88), who spent most of his life in Los Angeles, was regarded as a master craftsman and a quiet original by his teachers Robert Lowell and John Berryman, his peers Donald Justice, W.D. Snodgrass, Thom Gunn and Philip Levine, and his students Wanda Coleman, Michael Harper and Luis Omar Salinas. His first volume, *The War of the Secret Agents and Other Poems* (1966), won the Lamont Poetry Prize and received significant praise, but his second, *The Family Goldschmitt* (1971), was accidentally pulped by the distributor. A third volume only saw publication as part of his *Collected Poems* (1990), now long out of print.

Michael Caines works at the *Times Literary Supplement*. He is the author of *Shakespeare and the Eighteenth Century* (Oxford University Press, 2013) and the editor of a *TLS* bicentennial celebration of Jane Austen. He is writing a short book about literary prizes, and a slightly longer book about Brigid Brophy. He is founding editor of the *Brixton Review of Books*.

Boris Dralyuk is the author of *My Hollywood and Other Poems* (2022), editor of *1917: Stories and Poems from the Russian Revolution* (2016), co-editor of *The Penguin Book of Russian Poetry* (2015), and the translator of Isaac Babel, Andrey Kurkov and other authors. His poems, translations and criticism have appeared in the *New York Review of Books*, the *Times Literary Supplement*, *The New Yorker*, *The New Republic*, *Best American Poetry 2023* and elsewhere.

Henri Coulette

edited by Michael Caines and Boris Dralyuk

New and Selected Poems

CARCANET CLASSICS

First published in Great Britain in 2026 by
Carcanet
Main Library, The University of Manchester
Oxford Road, Manchester, M13 9PP
www.carcanet.co.uk

A CIP catalogue record for this book is
available from the British Library.

ISBN 978 1 80017 552 5

Book design by Andrew Latimer, Carcanet
Typesetting by LiteBook Prepress Services
Printed in Great Britain by SRP Ltd, Exeter, Devon

The publisher acknowledges financial
assistance from Arts Council England.

CONTENTS

from *The Family Goldschmitt*

from *And Come to Closure*

Uncollected Poems

It is a great irony that Henri Coulette, a poet of remarkable refinement and exquisite formal control—the son, no less, of a gifted musician—suffered from such terrible timing. Part of a cohort at the Iowa Writers' Workshop in the 1950s that included Philip Levine, W.D. Snodgrass, Donald Justice, and Robert Mezey, Coulette seemed destined to share the success of his peers in the decade ahead. Yet by the time his first collection, *The War of the Secret Agents and Other Poems*, won the Lamont Poetry Prize from the Academy of American Poets and appeared in 1966, the impeccably polished, wittily elegiac, ironically self-effacing poems it contained were distinctly out of fashion. In instead were the "confessional" mode pioneered by Snodgrass and adopted by their teachers at Iowa, Robert Lowell and John Berryman; the Beat howls emanating from San Francisco; the "open forms" Mezey and Stephen Berg would champion in their immensely popular anthology *Naked Poetry* (1969). To make things worse, most of the copies of Coulette's second collection, *The Family Goldschmitt* (1971), were accidentally pulped at the publisher's warehouse, ensuring that the book would fail to receive even the lukewarm reviews that greeted his debut.

Although he never stopped writing poems and continued to enjoy the friendship, admiration, and support of his better-known colleagues, Coulette published less and less. A proud Angeleno, he taught for decades at his alma mater, California State University—Los Angeles, mentoring poets such as Wanda Coleman, Michael S. Harper and Luis Omar Salinas, whose reputations would eventually eclipse his own. Increasingly alienated from the literary world and, in the last decade of his life, divorced from his beloved wife, he died in 1988, at 61, just as the New Formalism movement, in which he might have played a leading role, was gaining traction on the U.S. poetry scene. Not even in death would Coulette strike it lucky. A sumptuous

Collected Poems, lovingly compiled by Justice and Mezey in 1990, could have established his posthumous legacy, but it was savaged in print by Levine, once the closest of Coulette's friends, with whom he had fallen out at some point in the late 1970s.

In short, if you have not heard of Henri Coulette, it comes as no surprise to us. It is, however, a situation that ought to be remedied. His time has come. Poetry has always had its moods, whole climate shifts indeed, by which persisting in existing modes of form and thought may be dismissed as not just *démodé* but altogether redundant. Coulette belongs to that club of writers either widely ignored in their own era or working in willed obscurity whose original qualities nevertheless ought to ensure an enduring reputation. That *Collected Poems*, which long ago went out of print, testifies to his strikingly good ear and assured way with a variety of forms. The drama of "The War of the Secret Agents", a sequence reproduced in the present volume in its entirety, depends on a sharp sense of the interplay of competing voices; read such work out loud and you catch a sense of phrase unfolding from phrase, of repetition and variation, of ruminative, sometimes bleakly humorous verbal music. If there is despair here, it is elegantly done. A touch of Weldon Kees's black mood may be felt here more than once, but Coulette territory is, taken as a whole, something else, touched also by a sense of the absurd: it stretches from war-torn Europe and Renaissance England to his own backyard in Los Angeles, including not only Hollywood and scenes inspired by detective fiction (the crime novelist Ross Macdonald was a friend) but lesser-known corners of the city's suburbs and wry domestic interiors.

Another virtue: the reader should be wary of taking these evocations solely at face value. "The War of the Secret Agents", for example, takes inspiration from the misadventures of the British Special Operations Executive during the Second World War, from a world of codenames and shadowy identities;

it draws on Jean Overton Fuller's writings about SOE and its less fortunate agents in France, published during the 1950s. Coulette could attach another meaning to these wartime manoeuvrings, though. In an interview with Michael S. Harper, he characterises the sequence as "really a way I had of describing my neurosis", to "describe the way I saw the world". The spy's job of listening, watching, and keeping quiet had something fundamental in common with the passage from childhood to adulthood (a passage the young Coulette was still undertaking during the Second World War). In shorter poems, meanwhile, such as "Life with Mother" and "The Family Goldschmitt", identity remains unstable, ready to undergo a metamorphosis in the course of a few stanzas. The shock of history still reverberates through these poems, whether that means the perilous world of Henrician England, France in the wake of the Holocaust, or the U.S. under the political and cultural hammerblows of the 1960s. One kind of shock, however, may often disguise another, and the scale of the impact is implicit in the act of disguise itself.

*

We have tried, without a single quotation from his poems, to limn Coulette's mode, and that mode may already strike some readers as familiar. An obsession with disguises, a magpie's hunger for obscure sources plucked from every stratum of culture, a gift for dramatic counterpoint, for allusions intricate yet lightly worn, for mimicry that enriches without erasing the poet's personality—these are the stock-in-trade of T.S. Eliot, who, in his (fictional) role as Overton Fuller's editor at Faber, makes a cameo appearance in "The War of the Secret Agents". Yet Coulette wasn't merely playing Possum. His own four-piece suit was of an original cut, fashioned, as he suggested to Harper, by the neurotic insecurities stemming from an unstable childhood in a home full of secrets.

According to his birth certificate, Henri Coulette was born in Los Angeles on 11 November 1927 to Robert Roger Coulette, a professional musician and teacher, then 47, and Genevieve Reilly, a housewife, then 38. He was a late child, the last of three sons. The certificate lists his name as Henry—which is how he pronounced it all his life, preferring to be called Hank. The Frenchified spelling was one of the family's affectations, an imposed disguise to which he had to get accustomed early. The most pronounced inaccuracy on the form, however, concerns his father, who is listed as a native of Indiana. A secret of which the younger Coulette was likely aware, but which he didn't reveal even to his wife, is that Robert Roger Coulette had been born in Italy as Rosario Ruggiero Culotta, immigrating to the United States in the late 1890s. He changed his name sometime before settling in Fort Wayne, Indiana, in the early years of the new century. At that time, Italians were far less welcome in the U.S. heartland than were the French, and the new moniker helped Coulette establish himself as a sought-after musician and man about town. It might also have helped him secure permission to marry Genevieve Reilly, the young daughter of a successful Irish-American family, in 1908. Their son proudly embraced his mother's heritage, claiming that even the Coulette name was of Irish origin. In truth, his father was not naturalized until 1937, on the eve of a war that would see 600,000 Italian-Americans declared "enemy aliens".

The Coulettes moved to Los Angeles in the 1920s, where Robert found work as a musician at local theatres and on the radio, while Genevieve fell under the spell of various Theosophical offshoots and scams then proliferating in the city. "She is being watched by agents of the Kremlin", Coulette writes in "Life with Mother":

an agent herself
of the Ascended Masters,
she knows, she knows. St. Germain is here,
now, in this room. See, the light bulb is blinking!

There were profound tensions in the family, at which another poem, "The Invisible Father", hints even more clearly:

> One of us said, once, that you stood
> On the dark side of Mother.
>
> I think now that you stood
> Behind us, like the sun,
>
> Fathering our shadows toward her.
> You have become the music
>
> You practiced hours and hours
> Elsewhere in that strange house,
>
> The difficult passage I hear
> Suddenly in context.

"Elsewhere" seems to have served as a shibboleth for Coulette, "[a] password to some secret, inner place" ("Night Thoughts"). "The power of love is spoken of elsewhere", he writes in "Elsewhere", the second of two brilliant poems inspired by the case of Dennis Farrell, a traumatized veteran of the Second World War, "Gaunt Crusoe of a nowhere isle" who lived rough on the hillsides of L.A.'s sprawling Griffith Park from 1953 to 1959. The realm where love is spoken of is so closely guarded that, in the poet's most piercing lyrics, even the passwords fail. The speaker is left with his "oceanic longings" ("The Black Angel"), seeking another point of entry. But what beauty there is in the quest. Donald Justice captures the effect with Coulettian precision and poignancy in his poem for his dear friend, "Portrait with Flashlight", which begins:

> What lonely aisles you prowled
> In search of the forbidden,

Blinking your usher's torch,
Firefly of the balconies!

One couldn't blame the young Coulette for looking elsewhere as his parents' marriage disintegrated in the 1930s. At the age of 13, he moved with his mother and older brother to Santa Fe, New Mexico, where he began high school but was soon forced to drop out and take a job in order to support the fractured family. It was then, Coulette told Harper, that he "found out one of the ways that you survive is to keep your mouth shut. You become a secret agent. You don't let people know what you're thinking or feeling, because if you do, they'll fire you."

A voracious reader, Coulette didn't resume his formal education until after his year-long service in the Second World War. He was just old enough to enlist in 1945, and was on leave in Los Angeles, where his parents had reconciled a few years earlier, when his father died in his arms. He enrolled in Cal State LA, which was founded in 1947, and joined the bohemian circle of poets, writers, and artists that had formed around the charismatic leftist poet Thomas McGrath, who was dismissed from his post at the university in 1953 after appearing as an unfriendly witness before the House Un-American Activities Committee—another reminder, if Coulette needed any, that revealing what one is thinking or feeling too directly comes at a cost.

By then Coulette was a married man, having wed Jacqueline Meredith in 1950, and in Iowa. In 1952, he was offered a fellowship at the Writers' Workshop by its visionary director, Paul Engle, "on the strength", Coulette recalled in a late reminiscence titled "So Began the Happiest Years of My Life", "of a handful of poems he—and I think he alone—saw any strength or touch of talent in." In reality, his early poems, some of which had already appeared in print, would have struck anyone as promising, but the sharpening of his skills is evident in his 1954 Master's thesis, *The Hidden Man*, and his 1959 Doctoral thesis, *The Attic*, much of which would appear in his first book.

With the dissertation filed, Coulette returned to Cal State LA, to take up a teaching post—and there he remained, throwing himself into his work and the life of the English department, known for his smart personal dress code and penchant for a fast car. The place suited him. It was there he crossed paths with the British writer Christopher Isherwood, who thought him "really sweet and bright and full of quiet but powerful passion", and put a cameo portrait of him into his novel *A Single Man* (1964). Thom Gunn could recollect, in 1975, that it was "Hank Coulette" who had organized the state college's "first poetry reading ever"; the unsophisticated audience, faced with Berryman, Gunn et al, "insisted on clapping between each poem", but "largely due to Hank's influence" they had matured greatly.

Writing poetry, meanwhile, was taking place against a thoroughly Californian backdrop. Aside from the pedagogy (for which Coulette would be named Cal State's "Outstanding Professor of the Year" in 1970), there was the journal *Statement*; his local radio show about poetry on KPFK; his friendship with the crime writer Ross Macdonald (né Kenneth Millar), who took the title for the last of his Lew Archer novels, *The Blue Hammer* (1976), from Coulette's "Confiteor" ("and the blue vein, that small hammer at the wrist"); an enduring fascination with the movies (one sees it in the early poem "In Praise of Clowns", published here for the first time, and the fine late poem, "The Extras"); an equally lasting passion for sport. Poems that made their way into that first published collection, *The War of the Secret Agents*, take note of the "slums of Pasadena" ("The Blue-Eyed Precinct Worker") and the presence of a rival poet in the form of a machine developed in Glendale in the 1950s ("Lines for LBG-30, Computer, Poet"):

> I must envy you, for see
> how this hand trembles among
> these half-finished, abandoned
>
> odes, how migraine dulls the eye
> that looks on them...

If I feed you my sick lines,
will your indifference clean
and polish and complete them?

Various in its sources of inspiration and virtuosic in its variety of form, the book was awarded the Lamont for 1965, when the judges were James Dickey, Anthony Hecht, Louis Simpson, W. D. Snodgrass and May Swenson. Snodgrass, in particular, having come to know the younger poet at Iowa, seems to have been significantly impressed by the sequence that gave *The War of the Secret Agents* its title: he cited it as an influence, alongside Theodore Weiss's *Gunsight*, on his own search for a way of pitting one voice against another to create a greater whole (a search that would eventually lead to Snodgrass's controversial cycle, *The Führer Bunker*). Here Coulette had created what Snodgrass termed a "voice-collision" by dramatizing the shadowy situation of Overton Fuller's *Double Webs: Light on the Secret Agents' War in France* (1958) and, as mentioned above, imbuing it with something of his own insights into the subterfuges of everyday life. Although there were some encouraging reviews for the collection as a whole (with one *New York Times* critic being put in mind of the "best work of Wallace Stevens" and another hailing Coulette as "a poet to watch"), this sequence left a couple of reviewers cold. Denis Donoghue evinced especial laziness as a poetry critic when he declared himself to be "stumped", in the *New York Review of Books*, by "Orphan Annie: The Broken Code", the shortest part of the sequence, which consists of six lines of numerals. While we won't spoil its secret here, we can hardly pretend that the code requires a great deal of mental effort to crack.

Readers who take the trouble to read "The War of the Secret Agents" slowly (out loud, even) stand a better chance than Donoghue did of appreciating Coulette's artful handling of the stories of people who were, from the historical point of view, mere "footnotes with beautiful names", "passports without photos". They will see why Stephen Yenser called the cycle "captivating, emanating mystery".

Coulette states in *The War of the Secret Agents* that the book is arranged in five sections, in "simply chronological order". His second collection, *The Family Goldschmitt*, likewise consists of five sections—or acts, perhaps, given the dramatic addition of a prologue and an epilogue—but also an altogether more ambitious structure. According to the dust jacket, its subject is "modern American experience—in Europe and at home". Recent events play out in this vast arena, perhaps most obviously in the poems that allude to the political assassinations on American soil during the 1960s; but Coulette's family history runs through the collection, too, in poems such as "The Invisible Father" (quoted above), as well as telling incidents such as the one which inspired the title poem:

> Punctual as bad luck,
> The aerogramme comes sliding
> Under the door, mornings,
> Addressed to the Family Goldschmitt.
> My landlady puts it there.

This landlady "Insists that I am Goldschmitt":

> Coulette, I tell her, Coulette,
> Fumbling my money-green passport.
> I'm American, gentile,
> And there's gas escaping somewhere!
> She nods and mutters, Goldschmitt.

A misdirected message, slipped under the door of the room in Copenhagen where the Coulettes had been staying while waiting for cheques to arrive, is here transformed into something with far more sinister implications, akin to the disquieting spirit of Arthur Miller's novel *Focus* (1945) or Joseph Losey's film *Monsieur Klein*

(1976), in both of which a gentile is mistaken for a Jew, to terrible effect. It is all too easy to be out of step with history in *The Family Goldschmitt*, or even to find oneself going in the opposite direction to everyone else, as in "Walking Backwards" ("The horizon follows me. / The tall buildings lurch by"). The body itself keeps its secrets compartmentalized, as in "Portrait of the Left Hand" (first published in the *New Yorker*):

> The runt of a litter of two,
> It has never been housebroken,
> Retrieves only the small evils:
>
> The drink, the smoke, the pill.
> Even in the act of love,
> It wanders away, bored.

With this book, Coulette found himself, in turn, out of step with the times. *The Family Goldschmitt* boasted an endorsement from Zbigniew Herbert, lauding it as the work of "enduring value" by a "major poet, one in complete control of the technical resources of his art". Not many other readers had the opportunity to judge the book for themselves, however, given its dismaying fate at the hands of its own publisher.

Yet more dismayingly, Coulette seems to have let the book's mangled publication and reception get the better of him. His drinking grew worse, and by the end of the decade his marriage was over. Poems continued to appear sporadically into the 1980s, largely in the *The New Criterion*, a journal that championed formal verse, but there was no attempt to save *The Family Goldschmitt* from neglect. It was only after Coulette's death that Donald Justice and Robert Mezey, with the help of the poet's nephew, William Patrick O'Reilly, discovered that a third manuscript, *And Come to Closure*, had been completed. It sat in a box in his closet, another secret.

Justice and Mezey's *The Collected Poems of Henri Coulette* appeared on fine paper, under handsome covers, from the University of Arkansas Press in 1990, but the occasion, which should have begun a revival, was spoiled by Philip Levine, then at the height of his influence, who took the opportunity to settle old scores in print. In four letters to the editor of the journal *Common Knowledge*, he at first refused to review the book, though he and Coulette had been "brothers in this art", then complimented his old friend backhandedly, then withdrew even those words of spiteful praise, his view supposedly corrected by a younger poet on his death bed, who found nothing to like in the book. Coulette's more loyal friends and admirers, including Justice, Mezey, Snodgrass, Robert Dana, Edgar Bowers, Timothy Steele and a half-dozen others, took to the pages of *The New Criterion*, with a statement of "indignation and sorrow", but the damage had been done.

There is something as fittingly Coulettian about that posthumous stab in the back as there is about the hidden manuscript. Readers of this collection will discover a poet who would have accepted the sting with a rueful shrug. "The dead are dead", one of his secret agents scribbled on the back of an envelope, "and we live out the new lies, / without love, beyond betrayal." Not, we hasten to correct the statement, entirely without love, for Coulette's work has inspired precisely that feeling in us for many years, and we hope you will come to feel the same.

INTAGLIO

I have a picture in my room in which
Four gawky children strike a pose and stare
Out at the world without a worldly care.
Three girls and a boy in a paper hat:
The one too much a mouse to be a bitch,
The bitch, the actress, and the acrobat.

The roles I give them, half suggested by
The poses that they took, are meaningless,
For they are playing games. It is recess
Or summer—we have interrupted them.
They pose for us, with Agile romping by
And dark-eyed Pensive plucking at her hem.

This is my family. I dust them now
And then, and they return the courtesy
By never growing up. Thus, irony
Becomes a kind of family likeness, treasured
Not for the casual sameness of a brow
But for the attitudes one's mind has measured.

I knew an Agile once. To prove himself
The nimbler one, he pushed his books aside,
And crossed to Europe and the war, and died,
And his agility, which I believed a power
Then, then was gone, and his books on my shelf
Harvest the sunlit dust, hour after hour.

And there was Pensive, too, and everything
She touched was touched with fear. She married well,
Her people said, but marriage proves a hell
For those who marry but the flesh alone.
Who would have known a turn of mind could bring
Such knowledge to a girl? Who would have known?

I think of her, the child with heavy heart,
Heavy with child, and, Child, I think of you
And all the follies you will journey through;
I know them as an author knows his book.
Action and thought are nothing if apart.
Love in a gesture, wisdom in a look—

These are the real births for which we die.
Outside, the neighbor children startle me,
Calling *Allee, alleeoutsinfree.*
They cut for home. I hear a whirring skate
Fading through the darkness like a sigh.
I dust the frame and set the picture straight.

THE ATTIC

We have ascended to this paradise,
Make-believe angels hurrying to our choirs.
Imagination is our Sunday vice;
We are alone, alone with our desires.

We are enchanted by the sound of rain;
Darkness, half-light, and light combine and blur.
This is the national treasury of Cockaigne,
Of which we are the keepers, as it were.

Time is our Midas. We are of his line;
His touch descends to us on either side
—That golden touch. One gesture will refine
This dust into such realms as dust would hide.

These beads are pearls disguised as imitations.
This broken chair, my dear? It is a throne
From which you may survey the lesser nations,
Those lands that cannot claim you as their own.

This box contains the music of the spheres;
Its Swiss machinery records the stars.
Ever the listener given to fancy hears
The strings of Venus and the drum of Mars.

Time and Imagination—what are they?
They are, my dear, the pseudonyms of Change,
The smooth, indifferent author of our play,
Master of both the common and the strange.

My sister, it is autumn in Cockaigne,
And we are weary, for we've come so far
—Too far to be enchanted by the rain.
We are alone, alone with what we are.

The pride of wrights, the joy of smiths abide
        In fallen things—
      In tattered carpetings,
    In blackamoors and chamber pots.
Useless, they stay there in their show of pride
       Under the naked watts.

Is that not childhood in the corner there,
        Color and riot
      So dark now, and so quiet?
    To linger there would be unwise.
What if the tongues of wagons beat the air,
       And dolls opened their eyes?

O milliners, I see you in the hats
        Your deftness made,
      Imprisoned in their shade.
    I mark the cartwheel and the sailor,
The toque, the cloche—these are your habitats,
       Eternity your jailer.

The shoe forsaken is essential last.
        The cobbler fled
      Barefooted with the dead;
    His cunning stayed upon the sole.
Poor boot, your consolation is your past—
       Now broken, you are whole.

Medusa must have looked upon these clocks.
        They are so still,
        With no time left to kill.
    They are like chimneys without lamps
Or keys forever separate from their locks;
        They are like cancelled stamps.

Ah, this is the imperium of things,
        Things in themselves.
    These crammed and dusty shelves
    Contain us in the things we wrought.
These bronze, unbarbered heads are not our kings
        But subjects of our thought.

Where are the people as beautiful as poems,
As calm as mirrors,
With their oceanic longings—
The idler whom reflection loved,
The woman with the iridescent brow?
For I would bring them flowers.

I think of that friend too much moved by music
Who turned to games
And made a game of boredom,
Of that one too much moved by faces
Who turned his face to the wall, and of that marvelous liar
Who turned at last to truth.

They are the past of what was always future.
They speak in tongues,
Silently, about nothing.
They are like old streetcars buried at sea,
In the wrong element, with no place to go…
I will not meet *her* eye,

Although I shall, but here's a butterfly,
And a white flower,
And the moon rising on my nail.
This is the presence of things present,
Where flying woefully is like closing sweetly,
And there is nothing else.

Winged Victory of Nowhere,
the dressmaker's dummy stood,
guarding the hive in the harp.

Like a string of topaz beads
or a brassy abacus,
the bees flew their sweet missions.

The broken attic window
let them in. A safe distance
away, we watched and wondered.

You seemed intent on the bees,
their dances, how they hovered,
the fingerprints of Midas,

and I thought about the harp,
how it stood in a strange way
for all my lost occasions.

We went downstairs silently,
and made love, and later on
called someone to clean them out.

DOUBLEWALKER

You will find me occasionally, there, with you—
the lone shoe in the fast lane
of the freeway, the anonymous key
among your collar studs—
or your hairpins, as the case may be.

I am the factory reject. I inhabit
your daydreams, your nightwatches—
I come on, like something from Dick Tracy.
You have heard the bugles
of the Chinese infantry, perhaps?

I was the bugler. If I bear no resemblance
to my photograph, you know,
nevertheless, the look of me: the dark
mirror calls me Omar,
Omar, and it holds us in its arms.

Remember those gentle kooks
who would stand at the crossroads,
directing traffic, Sundays?

And Grandfather Patterson
in his rocker, whistling down
the beagle in the painting?

And the blind Negress who talked
to herself in a language
all her own, at the corner?

They have disappeared, stealing
the ice cards out of windows,
the cloth fronts of radios.

We tolerated much, once.
Grass grew through our cracked sidewalks,
and the rag man cried and cried.

This is the last retreat that Graciousness
      Can call her own.
     It stands in brick and stone,
    Victorian to the very eaves,
But for the servants who, I must confess,
      Are bloody modern thieves.

The daughters of the noble and the rich
      Are finished here.
     What polish, what veneer!
    These Helens have their father's nod:
Ledeans know by instinct which is which;
      They know the bill of God.

They learn here what is pleasing to a man.
      From stock exchange
     To modern art they range;
    Of ancient houses, recent horses,
They know the names; and of the Aga Khan,
      The size of his resources.

I ask you, Mrs. Rennie-O'Mahony,
      You, the Queen Swan,
     Inform me if you can
    What cygnets dream of when they sleep.
Is it the wrinkled faces found on money?
      And do the cygnets weep?

Ignore the beggar, kick the sycophant,
          I love the class
          That paddles on its ass!
        The Begum comes, if Aga can;
And if he can't, the Begum speaks of Kant,
          Or quotes the Alcoran.

It will be summer, spring, or fall—
Or winter, even. Who would know?
For no one answers when we call
Who might have answered years ago.

The harvest will be in or not;
The trees in flower or in rime.
Indifferent to the cold, the hot,
We will no longer care for time.

Mortal, of ivory and of horn,
We will become as open gates
Through which our nothing will be borne,
By which all nothing now but waits.

It will be summer, spring, or fall—
Or winter, even. Who will care?
We will not answer when you call,
For nothing, nothing echoes there.

You are a mother-in-law
and suffer from hot flashes;
you are an eight-year-old boy
with wide blue eyes and a scar
on your right knee; you are mad
with ambition, and forty,
a man to be counted on.
You are my enemy, O.K.?

You get around. You turn up
in everybody's mirror,
naked. You are a best seller;
the blind are fingering you.
You have become Tchaikovsky;
even the deaf turn you on.
Now you call yourself Scandal
—and sleep with Hyperbole!—

who once lay silent, at ease
in my arms, behind these blinds.
You had only one smile then.
You were, of course, too perfect;
you scared me, and I went out
with you on my arm. Today,
I must mourn a love buried
in the gaze of passers-by.

LIFE WITH MOTHER

Everything's left to the imagination,
Mother says, and winks
an eye, green and beautiful.
I nod encouragement, and wink back,
imagining myself anywhere but here,
in this room, with this woman.

She has been very famous in her lifetimes—
Queen Elizabeth,
Alexander Hamilton—
this poor Irish daughter of the man
who invented the Nabisco fig newton,
this woman who has no friends.

She is being watched by agents of the Kremlin;
an agent herself
of the Ascended Masters,
she knows, she knows. St. Germain is here,
now, in this room. See, the light bulb is blinking!
K-17 is here too,

and the Lord Kathumi is in the kitchen.
I nod, I must nod,
or be a Black Magician.
And if I did speak, what could I say?
There are ashes on all your sidewalks, Mother.
There are ashes in my mouth.

THE SICKNESS OF FRIENDS

Do I give off in the wee,
small hours a phosphorescent
glow, perhaps, like rotting wood?

Am I in the Yellow Pages?
I am sick of the sickness
within me that so lures them

to their phones when the night stops
in a dead calm: "H'llo." It's Dick,
who can't bear to be alone;

or Jane, who needs a father;
or Spot, who leads a dog's life.
Even the operator

has twin raw scars on her wrists,
but I'm fine, unmarked, floating
in the bath of their self-love.

CHICKEN RAMPANT, BAR SINISTER

I tell him my thirteen secret names,
and I say,
"All my decisions are committee decisions,
and some of my selves,
Doctor, are always out of town."

Rich as Onassis, I count my fears.
In my dreams
I see the hard-hearted and familiar strangers
circling around me,
and I don't know if I'm their king

or their victim. Chicken rampant, bar
sinister—
my family coat of arms hangs, invisible,
in an empty room.
Memory's a form of simile:

I am like all my unknown and frightened fathers.

BITTER SUITE

I. THE REPROACH

Observe how life reproaches art:
I, who was lonely in the crowd,
And took my loneliness to heart,
Would now be lonely if allowed.

II. DECEMBER

Of passion there is little said,
For he would have you think him cold,
Whom passion would not leave for dead,
Though reason found him far too old.

III. NEXT QUESTION

Oh, who is Goober, what is he?
Inquires the peanut of the pea.
And, thus, the candle to the wick,
Why, Goober, Brightness, is a prick.

IV. THE GUTLESS WONDER

Dapper I perceive:
Clothes upon a peg:
Nothing up his sleeve,
Nothing down his leg.

V. QUEER AT EASY

Where is it that the wise abide?
What houses and what streets are theirs?
Nowhere! Nowhere! The wise have died,
In joy, in silence, without heirs.

VI. ROBERT ROGER COULETTE, MUSICIAN

He plays no more
Whose play was need,
The darkened score,
The broken reed.

I: EVENING IN THE PARK

The children have packed up the light
And gone home for the bedtime story
In which Jack wakes the Sleeping Fury.
I count tin cans and comic books;
I listen for the wheel of night,
That furry rim, those velvet spokes.

Some know it by the rush of stars;
I know it by the rush of thought:
Images, like the shrill onslaught
Of cyclists on a black-top road,
Come on and catch me unawares:
I am the victim of their mood.

It is a rehash of the day,
The rooms remembered for their anger,
The crowded stairways for their danger,
And what the light did to a mirror
You thought you knew. It is a way
Of being faithful to one's terror.

I will sit here a little while,
Recalling how I read about
A man who found a strange way out,
The hermit of this wooded park,
Gaunt Crusoe of a nowhere isle,
Who hides his bushel in the dark.

He may be watching even now,
His dark hands up his darker sleeves,
The last of the great make-believes.
He moves in an enormous grave,
The wilderness pressed to his brow,
A man of motion without drive.

I wonder, Does he name the trees?
And to what end? Or like a bird,
Does he know calls that know no word?
And does he conjure without number?
And when, against the moon, he sees
My silhouette, does he remember?

Batman is whispering in the wind;
The cans are jewelled with the stars,
Evening Venus and red-eyed Mars.
I am an eight-hour daylight man,
And I must go to keep my mind
Familiar and American.

I have loved you foolishly, my unaltered
ego, as children
love an invisible friend.
Your Purple Heart and honest parents
were the very things to leave, and if you had
a secret wound, it was

a harbor where the darkness rode at anchor
in imperial calm.
And you had gone; I could stand
on the back porch, the television
voices all around me in the dark, and think
you out there, or mistake

a low star for your campfire, and feel the heat.
Yet, for all I know,
it was I who drew you down,
so friendly, dog-like, among the cops,
the bald psychiatrist, the weeping parents,
the man from Channel 2.

The power of love is spoken of elsewhere.
I note in passing
only how cold the nights are
of late, though, they are not, I suppose,
as cold as the night you have where they have you,
at home, in Nebraska.

I gave them bad habits and impossible loves.
I was arrogant,
heavy with ambition, sad.
They were footnotes with beautiful names;
they were passports without photos; they were dust,
and I took that dust in hand.

JANE ALABASTER   a scholar who is writing a history
of secret agents
in France during World War II.
She is concerned that many of them
survive only under a cloud of treason.
The lady is a spinster.

PROSPER   the chief of the secret agents in Paris;
captured by Kieffer,
he agrees to a deal whereby,
surrendering his agents, he gains
the promise from Kieffer of their safekeeping;
he has a wife named NANCY.

ARCHAMBAULT   He is Prosper's radio operator,
has red hair, very
strange eyes, and writes bad poems.
His Christian name (Gilbert) when
pronounced
in the French manner by Denise rimes
with that
of the following agent:

HILAIRE PENTECÔTE   who bears a most remarkable resemblance
to a famous star
of the French screen. Everything
passes through his hands, as he is Air
Movements Officer for the secret agents.
He has no truck with doctors.

DENISE	Prosper's courier and Archambault's mistress, she has a sister, an identical twin named DESIRÉE, who, though not an agent, concerns herself to the point of obsession with their comings and goings.
CINEMA, PHONO	These two are among the surviving agents: Cinema the Mad, a rider on the Métro, who becomes a lighthouse keeper; big Phono, a Piccadilly Lazarus, who finds himself—in a tall glass.
BUCKMASTER	the London head of Special Operations Executive (or the S.O.E. or the Firm), an organization consisting of such amateurs as Prosper. BODDINGTON is his second in command.
THE GERMANS	KIEFFER, the head of the Paris Gestapo, who kept his promise as long as promises could be kept; WULF, his second in command, who ends as a mental patient; and YEAGER, a member of the *Wehrmacht*.
THE OTHERS	MAMA BEE is a famous American medium who tries to contact Prosper. MADAME GUEPIN, an ex-Resistance member. THE ABBÉ OF ARDON, a scholar. T.S. ELIOT, an editor.

Prosper, Archambault, Gilbert, and Cinema—
romantic code-names
out of a teen-age novel
(*The Motor Boys and the Gestapo*) —
who can remain unmoved at the wedding
of youth and propaganda?

And so with their transmitters they came to France,
gifted amateurs
ready to die for England
and the S.O.E. How could they know
that what London told them was a nightmare
London had from Hollywood?

They will appeal to lovers of the absurd:
there they were, bulging
with codes and automatics.
Like debutantes slumming on Skid Row,
they couldn't be missed—they advertised
and Death reads all the papers.

II. JANE ALABASTER: A LETTER TO T.S. ELIOT

Dearest Possum,
                    It is as if I wrote you
not from this Paris,
the capital of the Franks,
but from another, from a city
thrice more ancient, where gargoyles lean and leer
from parapets more subtle,

the ultimate prospect, ultimate Paris.
The quest is over!
Now the last chapter: Gilbert
has promised to meet me—"to explain"—
as if explanation were still possible.
Now to confront him at last!

Do you realize I have spent some five years
with the words of ghosts,
in the company of men
who, if they were not ghosts, were more mad,
more broken than we imagine men can be
and still be men and not ghosts?

The quest is over, with what joy! what sadness!
Five years of my life
in order to crown my life—
well, surely, it was worth it, Possum.
Faber and Faber, you shall have your manuscript,
And I shall have my laurels—

and what laurels, too! for my text is human.
I have established
the reading of what moves,
breathes, and has known too much suffering.
Forgive me, dear friend, if I brag a little.
Tomorrow I am forty

and tomorrow in the Place de la Concorde
I will meet Gilbert;
and meeting him, I will count
forty not as lonely women do
but as poets count their strophes, with a sense
of the timeless and the true.

11 November 1944—
I had one motive,
comfort, and I ended up
on a cold floor. I had one virtue,
loyalty, and I carried it far too far.
Goodbye, Goldilocks. Goodbye.

IV. KIEFFER'S DIARY: 1942-45: EXCERPTS[1]

1.

It is like a musical composition
without music, pure
as music can never be,
or a monstrous, new form of blindfold
chess, where the moves are all Byzantine, unknown.
Am I mad from paper-work?

2.

I find myself indifferent to places.
Paris means nothing;
Germany is forgotten.
I care only for the quirks of men.
Indeed, I study even the guards: brute Slavs,
dim Rumanian lackeys.

---

1 S.S. Sturmbannführer Hans Otto Kieffer
   counted beautiful
   women, good food, and sports cars
   among his passions, yet this diary,
   found after his execution, indicates
   a man of more than passion.

3.

What a beautiful, evil son of a bitch
Gilbert proves himself!
Photostats of Prosper's
reports to London clutter my desk.
He writes with such style that my English improves.
Is there a style for pity?

4.

I begin to know Prosper and his comrades.
There are even times
when I can sense their terror;
it is as though I were watching, too,
gazing up at my own office, at this light,
myself gazing at myself.

5.

What was an amusement is now a danger.
Africa, Russia—
what I delayed must begin:
we will come in the night like bad dreams.
I look forward to meeting them, as I might
the authors of my childhood.

6.

Name: Francis Suttill alias Prosper;
name: Gilbert Norman
alias Archambault; name:
Andrée Borrel alias Denise—
the shepherd has been introduced to his flock.
How shall I use my poor sheep?

7.

A long talk with Prosper—I have given him
my formal promise:
no harm will come to his men,
none at all, if he cooperates.
He is as honest as a cavalryman;
London has sent me a child.

8.

We two are caught up in a dream of pity.
We sit together
nodding over his reports,
his letters to his wife. Sleepwalker,
London was your God, and God has betrayed you.
You have my word, my pity.

9.

He consents!

10.

           We have bagged over a thousand.
They are in the net,
and not one drop of blood spilt.
What a beautiful, evil Gilbert—
to have given me so many charming birds,
to have given me their songs!

11.

A little treatise on the uses of song,
on the radio game?
London responds, arming us.
Yes, yes, they are sending us arms,
and I am sending messages to their wives.
Dear God, the uses of song!

12.

London has sent us a Major Boddington,
whom we wined and dined
and sent back in ignorance;
four commandoes whom we had to kill.
So blood has been spilt, so I must ask myself,
How can we lose? and still lose.

13.

Wulf and I have been trying to burn records;
there are too many.
And my lost sheep, where are they?
Exhausted beyond caring, we laugh,
hearing the festival of guns in the street,
in the Bois de Boulogne.

14.

They say I am to be hanged. I don't know why.
The four commandoes?
No, it is that they fear me,
that they fear what I don't know I know.
They fear what I might say, yet I would not speak:
the methods… the methods go on…

1. COLONEL BUCKMASTER

Truth, madam, is a waif in the wilderness—
it dies of neglect.
We have chosen to forget,
deliberately, out of kindness.
Truth is, Archambault was the English Judas
we have chosen to forget.

2. COLONEL YEAGER

The retreat from Paris was an Olympics
for half-mad cripples.
We limped and raved across France,
the great jaw of Chaos at our heels.
Germany had no time for Kieffer's promise;
she was preparing to die.

3. MADAME GUEPIN

Denise in the prison at Fresnes told me,
—*Gilbert me protège.*
She told me this, yes, and this,
—*C'est Gilbert qui nous a tous vendus.*
The dead are dead, and we live out the new lies,
without love, beyond betrayal.

VI. A PAGE FROM AN OFFICIAL HISTORY BY THE ABBÉ OF ARDON

Her sister, hearing of her imprisonment,
confronted the Boche
and begged to be made captive,
though innocent of Denise's crime.
Whatever their motive, they complied.
The Lord have mercy on her.

They came finally to the Natzweiler Camp,
where the sick were gassed,
and her sister being ill,
Denise begged to be chosen as well.
Thus, these daughters of France came to embrace Death.
The Lord have mercy on them.

I admire the driven, those who rise from choice
as from a sick bed.
I was of that company,
as you are, as he is whom you seek.
What little I know you must know, or have guessed.
Prosper, I assume, is dead;

we last met beside the train that had brought us
into Germany.
We came upon each other
in the steam of the brakes, and his eyes
were those of a blindman or a cuckold. We passed
each other without speaking.

The other one I met once on an airfield
my first night in France.
If I remember rightly,
we did not speak; perhaps we nodded;
perhaps his hand touched my elbow. I recall
only the scent of the cut hay

and the overwhelming sensual delight
I knew momently
under the dangerous moon.
Your prey was of the breathing darkness
wherein, without father, Cinema was born—
he was midwife at that birth.

A ghost of a cockney with a gift of tongues,
what did I become?
Whatever Cinema did,
and he did it well. And when I slept,
I could hear the nations underneath my ear,
and my dreams were of pure light.

This has the ring of nonsense about it, no?
How can I tell you?
How can I explain to one
never there? I was a courier
and rode the Métro, disguised differently
everyday. I was no one,

I was what I seemed, I did not have to think.
This house is the grave
of Cinema, and this light
his epitaph. How can I explain
the dead? The dead are an extravagant cheese,
nor have the sad gift of tongues.

The right frame of mind, honey, is a calm hope,
what Daddy Bee calls
"A Gentle Expectancy."
It's the practical approach to faith.
Now, my guide's a little Spanish spirit named
Guadalupe—you'll like her.

Let's begin… Guadalupe, Guadalupe,
can you hear me, dear?
Guadalupe, can you hear?
Am I getting through to you, honey?
We are trying to contact Major Suttill,
Major Francis Suttill, dear.

—*¿Como esta, Mama? ¿Que pasa? ¿Subtle who?*
No, Guadalupe,
it's Major Francis Suttill;
we think he passed over in the war.
Do you know him, honey, in the Great Beyond?
Honey, do you know him there?

(I am here. I wear the mufti of a shade.)
Is he there, honey?
Am I getting through to you?
(Mufti, and memory like a chain…)
Guadalupe, Guadalupe, are you there?
—*Vaya con Dios, Mama.*

IX. DENISE: A LETTER NEVER SENT

Desirée,
                          I find it most bitter that you,
my sister, my twin,
should set your heart against me.
Gilbert is my love, my protection—
I am no streetwalker in a scarlet sheath
tripping through the Place Pigalle.

How stupid, how petite-bourgeoise to unleash
such rabid, convent-
bred imaginings upon
me—your own sister, your twin!
I had thought to share the sweetness of my love.
How carefully I chose words!

I wanted so to tell you of this strange gift,
for I must conceive
of love as something given—
I wanted to tell you of Gilbert,
of how he crams my very being with such love,
and of his marvelous eyes.

Now you have come between me and my mirror.
How can I behold
my image—yes, our image—
without rancor? I must school myself
to be an only child, beyond reflection,
marvelous to his marvelous eyes.

The lost addresses of the soul are these:
the great estate
with mermaids at the gate
or the cold-water flat with wolves—
wherever loneliness like a disease
or a wildflower evolves—

or where like alabaster in the dark
she lies in wait
whom you would celebrate
in the exclusion of the mind,
whom you, in dreams, inchoate, know as ark,
crucible, and rind—

or where, powerful, irresponsible,
you turn away
from what the others say,
and—like a mirror come to life—
make of duplicity the single rule,
and use it like a knife.

XI. ORPHAN ANNIE: THE BROKEN CODE

8-9-12-1-9-18-5-16-5
14-20-5
3-15-20-5-9
19-1-4-15-21
2-12-5-1-7-5-14-20-6
15-18-11...

Thanks, I will.
                    You understand he wasn't mad?
even in the end?
Oh, I was there, I saw him,
I saw his mind become more lucid
hour by hour, thought by thought, lucid as the flesh
of the old, the very old,

a Chinese wisdom. I give you the Chinese.
I give you nothing
you can't find out for yourself,
except the last look of Archambault:
the delicate, livid face of a red-head,
with one brown eye, and one blue.

We knew at Mauthausen that we were to die.
My fear kept me sane;
I talked to it in my head.
Show these bastards how to die, I said.
My days were like dreams, in which I dreamt my death,
and lived like a coward.

And all the while Archambault lay there smiling
like a god damn saint.
There is nothing left to lose,
he said. *Nothing but my frigging life,*
I said, but he didn't hear me, or he heard
and knew there was nothing left.

Did you know, he laughed, *they captured us in bed,*
in Denise's bed?
I woke up with their torches
in my face. I dreamed they would be there,
and they were, and I wasn't afraid. I sighed,
I think, with satisfaction.

I rose, I stood stock still. I read the letter-
ing on the light bulb.
I saw Denise's nipples,
taut, purple, oddly oval. I heard
the embarrassed creaking of the German coats.
I smelled the oil on their guns.

I saw the world, and I gave back what I saw.
I was a mirror,
nothing more. I was faithful;
I gave an eye for an eye. Can they
execute a mirror? There will be gunfire
and an end to reflection.

—Show these Gothic bastards how to die, I said.
—You show them, he said,
and don't forget to say "cheese."
—Fuck your brown eye, and your blue, I said,
and in the morning, the guards took him outside
and shot him, and I waited,

knowing I would be next, saying, *Show them how…*
I waited nine months,
and the Americans came.
It was 80 days before I walked.
I was Lazarus come to Piccadilly,
unseeing, among strangers,

among the accusing Buckmasters of London,
among the whispers
of *treason, treason.—Bad show,*
a bad show best forgotten, old man,
Buckmaster said. He was embarrassed for me;
I had neglected to die.

It's madness, I know, but they wanted us dead.
Are the files neater
if you die? What Prosper did
when he dickered with that German crank
was to save a few lives—oh, not the best lives,
but a few; that was his crime.

And when you ask me why I drink, I must say
I don't know. Is it
in memory of Prosper,
of silly Prosper? Do I follow
Archambault by fifths, a brown eye, and a blue?
The Buckmasters of this world—

do I drink to stomach them? Or the coward
who waited nine months
and the Americans came?
Well, I give you the Americans.
Now one more for the road, and do count your change;
the publican is a cheat.

XIII. BUCKMASTER ON THE BBC

The rose is more than a handful of petals;
the hive is greater
than the meandering bee.
We are moved by, and toward, absolutes:
the rose for meaning, and the hive for purpose.
The rose, the hive, and Special

Operations Executive—or The Firm,
as we called it then—
what do they have in common?
Well, what is bravery without a cause?
How could any one of us fall asleep nights
without the rose and the hive?

XIV. WULF, AT THE ASYLUM

The doctors regard me as a classic case,
and that's the story
that I've doctored up for them,
or you, or any who come rooting
among my hems and haws. I'm a specialist;
I prescribe what you ask for,

and you ask for Kieffer. How will you have him?
wriggling on a rope?
or alone, the middle-aged
dandy, mooning over a desk lamp?
Kieffer, you know, could never cross his ankles
for fear of spoiling his shine:

we Germans have been seduced by our tailors.
We move, when we march,
in an ecstasy of tabs
and ribbons—the beautiful soldiers![2]
So Kieffer sat there at his great cherry desk,
his ankles never touching;

---

2   It must be noted that the speaker was not
    himself a soldier,
    for he belonged, like Kieffer,
    his superior, to the Gestapo,
    though that organization was properly
    known as the Sicherheitsdienst.

behind him, on the wall, framing his heavy,
military head,
the yellow map of Paris,
the tacks glistening like caught insects.
Gilbert stood among the shadows in the office,
and the shadows were like dark

angels landing and taking off. They whispered,
Gilbert and Kieffer,
or was it the sound of wings?
Desirée had turned against Denise,
as sisters turn against sisters in a world
carnivorous, but Kieffer

would delay, admiring his boots, and the tacks
glistened all night long.
Desirée was so lovely,
I could not believe she had a twin,
that that dark hair, those lost eyes, that crooked mouth
had any equals ever.

So Desirée came to Kieffer now and then,
and Kieffer would smile
as a parent smiles, hearing
a good lesson, and send her away.
This all happened a long time ago, and we
have all died, this way or that.

XV. PROSPER: A LETTER TO NANCY[3]

Le Sacré-Coeur trembles on the window pane,
a lorry rumbles
down the street, a baby cries
somewhere below stairs—who was it said,
Paris is for Englishmen and pickpockets;
lovers go to the country?

I am having one of my headaches today.
In a few minutes
the others will start arriving:
lumbering Phono, mad Cinema,
and the star-crossed lovers, of course. I must play
the greybeard for these children.

---

3   Nancy Suttill bas remarried. Her husband
     is a car salesman
     in Leeds. They have two children,
     a daughter and an adopted son;
     the son has been named Prosper—Prosper
     Pulkinghorn, to be exact.

     It is Nancy Pulkinghorn who has observed
     that this strange letter
     may be the work of Kieffer
     (see Section Eleven of Part Four).
     At this late date, she is unable to say
     more than this on this matter.

Their reports, as usual, will be worthless.
The Jerry troop train
is late. It is! It isn't!
But no, it has already arrived.
And then the arguments will start. Cinema
will storm out. Denise will cry.

When my cigarettes are gone, and my patience,
why, then they will leave,
and I will peer down at them,
there, on the street, and I will whisper,
God damn you, God damn you, I'm through, I've had it,
I'm going home to Nancy!

Then, I'll look around the room and see the flowers
Denise has brought me
for my desk. I'll arrange them,
giving them water, knowing I'll stay.
It is the thought of you that keeps me going,
but this is the way I go.

They were at a corner table in the Ritz.
Jean Gabin, she thought;
He looks just like Jean Gabin.
Hilaire had removed his dark glasses,
and his eyes were both wary and amused.
"You are Gilbert," she stated.

"No, I was Gilbert. I am Hilaire Pentecôte.
They are but two names
among many. There are names
on every side, waiting to be used;
I help myself. But what is it that you want?"
"You are Gilbert," she answered.

"I want justice. I confront you with your past."
"Ah, my dear lady,
you want justice in the Ritz?"
He made a soft gesture, and his hand
described the four-star luxury of the room.
"There were two of you," she said;

"The English Gilbert and the French Gilbert.
You are the latter,
the one of whom Denise said,
'C'est Gilbert qui nous a tous vendus.'
You sold them out, and a dead man got the blame."
"You are absolutely right,"

he said. "But what of it? What is it to you?"
"Just this," she answered:
"it wasn't Gilbert Norman,
and it wasn't that poor demented
girl, Desirée, either. My book will clear them."
"And label me a traitor?"

"Yes." "No," he answered; "that isn't possible."
"But it is. I can…"
"No," and he smiled; "no, you can't,
for I'm not the traitor that you think."
"But they gave the papers to you for the planes,
and you gave them to Kieffer,

"and Kieffer copied them, and gave them back…"
She was breathless now,
frightened by the innocence
that rode upon his smile. "Yes," he said,
"but I did only what London told me to—
I was London's instrument.

"There was an underground beneath the underground.
They protected it.
Kieffer never guessed the truth;
he was too busy counting the sheep
London let him have by way of sacrifice—
fifteen hundred little lambs!"

"No," she murmured, but she knew he spoke the truth.
It was as if truth
had an odor about it,
distinct, acrid as a camphor lamp.
"How do I know," she asked, "that you are not tell-
ing me an enormous lie?"

"You don't," he answered, and then he laughed. "Do you think
London will confirm
what I whisper in the Ritz?
No, but you can prove me innocent.
Write your book, and see if London prosecutes:
London will not lift a hand."

"Dear God," she said; "it is all too horrible:
fifteen hundred lives!"
"Yes," he said and touched her hand.
"It was no business for angels,
or sheep, or an Ivanhoe like our Prosper.
I am a religious man,

"and it grieves me." He said this almost shyly.
She looked at Hilaire.
"You have then a religion?"
"Yes," he said. "May I ask what it is?"
"Christian Science," he answered in a fine confusion.
"I am interested myself,"

she said, "in astrology. May I ask you
your chronology?
I have an ephemeris
in my bag." She took it from her purse.
"September 2, 1909,
at eleven in the night."

As he sipped his drink, a black currant syrup,
she drew a rough chart
on the back of the wine list.
"Your horoscope," she said, "is under
the dominance of an almost exactly
rising Neptune, and Neptune

"implies a taste for adventure—on all planes,
and in all senses,
embracing on the one hand
an aspiration toward the mystical,
and on the other, the mundane, a penchant
toward secret activities,

"with a liability toward duplicity.
I beg your pardon,
but it's here your drama lies,
especially as your planet's caught up
in a most spectacular grand-cross,
and a grand-cross, my dear sir,

"demands a working out in terms of violence."
He clutched the wine list
to him. "Now that," he said, "that
is fascinating. I mean really."
She smiled and nodded, and they sat silently
till the waiter brought the check.

Reader, we are getting ready to pull out.
Archambault has packed
the transmitter in an old
suitcase. Denise is combing her hair.
We are meeting Phono and Cinema downtown
in a second-rate bistro.

Prosper has been worrying about Phono;
he has a bad cough.
—And Cinema, I worry
about Cinema, who must insist
on a trenchcoat, of all things. But life goes on,
even here, in its own way.

Reader, you have been as patient as an agent
waiting at midnight
outside a deserted house
in a cold rain. You will ask yourself,
What does it all mean? What purpose does it serve,
my being here in this rain?

Reader (you will be known henceforth by that name),
there is no meaning
or purpose; only the codes.
So think of us, of Prosper, silly
Prosper, of Archambault of the marvelous eyes,
of Denise combing her hair.

My office partner dozes
at his desk, whimpering now
as he dreams his suicide.
The November light kisses
the scar of his last attempt.
I open my mail: a plea
for the starving Indian
children of North Dakota;

a special offer from *Time*,
Life, and *Fortune*; a letter
from a 65-year-old
former student, suggesting
a gland transplant that will make
a man of me; it hurts him
to hear what they are saying
about me behind my back.

It hurts me to hear what they
are saying to my face, pal.
I circle two misspelled words
and write, "Help I am being
held captive at Mickey Mouse
State College," across the top,
wondering, is this the one,
or the fat woman, perhaps,

with the post-menopause craze
for strict forms. "The sestina—
can you use any six words?"
Well, yes, but they should define
a circle, which is the shape
I describe, chasing my tail
from class to class, the straight line
disguised, degree by degree.

Liberal, blue-eyed, shivering, trying not
to look like a bill
collector or detective,
I move through the slums in a drizzle—
the slums of Pasadena, where—nutmeg, bronze,
and purple—the Negroes live.

They look out and laugh—Mrs. Bessie Simpson,
Miss Delilah Jones,
the eleven Tollivers.
They are extras in a bad movie
starring no one they have ever seen before,
no one that they care to know.

I am like a man rich in the currency
of a lost kingdom,
for this both is and is not
what I sought. Somewhere, a screen door bangs
and bangs, but in the half-light I can't see where,
or give the sound direction.

A black and white sausage of a mongrel bitch
follows me, sniffing;
her obscene stump of a tail
motionless. We go, the two of us,
to the muddy edge of the dark arroyo.
The street light blooms overhead;

our shadows burst forth monstrous and alien.
There, on the far rim,
are the houses of the rich.
It is the dinner hour, and they eat
prime rib of unicorn, or breast of phoenix.
It is another precinct.

Oddly enough, I am consoled by the thought
of the delicate
small animals that move down
through the arroyo: white coyote,
masked coon, and the plumed skunk. Come, Citizen Dog,
we have chosen the short straw.

AT THE TELEPHONE CLUB

We sit, crookbacked, at the bar,
each with his own telephone,
all of us with the same itch.
The tight-assed operator
in the opera stockings
—the only one worth having—
hovers, wisely, out of reach.
She has got all our numbers.

My phone rings: it's the matron
with lost eyes and a horse jaw.
I get rid of her: I have
an ugliness within me,
whole as I am not, a kind
of sleeping cancer. Who needs more?
I listen to the broken
English of an Amsterdam

blonde, seduced in her twelfth year—
it was summer!—by a man
in a Silver Cloud, but I
can have her now for the price
of a taxi ride. I can
have her in a Murphy bed,
while the roaches on the sink
stiffen their fine antennae.

I would, I would, dear lady,
but I have a plane to catch,
one piloted by a sly
Tibetan. I have a date
with some porters in the snow.
I buy her a Grasshopper,
and slip out into the night.
How cold the stars are, how clear!

LINES FOR LBG-30, COMPUTER, POET

So there you are in Glendale,
your circuits open and hot,
your dials iridescent—

the pure poet breaking through,
into pure nonsense, your own
tenth muse, inhuman, perfect.

I must envy you, for see
how this hand trembles among
these half-finished, abandoned

odes, how migraine dulls the eye
that looks on them. If sometimes
my worksheets stir and blossom,

airborne, they do so only
in that odd, recurring dream
wherein I dream my dying,

and see the whole world file past,
forgiving me, blessing me—
my mad mother, my good wife,

the poets I've stolen from,
the interminable strangers.
Dreamless, you go on and on.

If I feed you my sick lines,
will your indifference clean
and polish and complete them?

MINE

Surrounded by ancient *Lifes*,
chainsmoking, playing the role
I have come here not to play,

I think what a good poem
this will make, a modern one,
something suited to my style.

I store up details: fumbling
the five bills into the small
envelope delicately

handed to me, my quick check
of those hands to see they're clean,
his fifteen-minute story

of how he came to do time,
and is just out, how the place
may be bugged, how detectives

may approach me when I leave.
He goes back to her. Later,
she will tell me how he cleaned

the previous spring's birds' nests
from the air conditioner,
and chatted, while she rested;

and as she talks, I will be
surprised by my innocence,
and feel it die, and feel old.

Conceived in love and anger,
your dark mother crying, No!
what were you but a tiny

fist of blood that should have beat
against doors till one opened
and your father took you in?

Now you are these lines, these lines
I cannot put my name to,
or make good enough to live.

> *"Anything can happen in Thimble City,*
> *because you run it."*
>
> —ad for a Remco toy

A filling station, a car,
a skyscraper, and a house—
that's enough for any town.

The car, full of gasoline,
goes a hundred miles an hour,
but no one ever drives it.

Where's to go? The skyscraper
has a poet in every room,
and each poet is a school

unto himself. And the house?
The house is where the lovers
(meaning you, meaning me) live.

It is where we never hurt
each other, and is no place
I have been to or heard of.

He was one of us, surely,
for look what we have found here
in the corners where he lived:

unpaid bills, pornographic
playing cards, six love letters
with circles over the i's.

He pretended otherwise:
the photograph of Baudelaire,
the Burberry, the XK-E.

But there were times, and I speak
perhaps only personally,
when everything coalesced—

one time, we had been drinking
Chivas Regal all that night,
and the eucalyptus burned

in the fireplace, and the dawn,
or the false dawn—whichever
it was—lighted the hawk home,

he said, *When I have kicked off*
and they cut me open, they
will find a dime-store diamond,

worthless, but reflecting light
where the heart is said to be.
And when we cut, we found it.

THE FAMILY GOLDSCHMITT

Punctual as bad luck,
The aerogramme comes sliding
Under the door, mornings,
Addressed to the Family Goldschmitt.
My landlady puts it there.

My landlady—that blonde aura
Of everything Nordic, Clairol
And kroner, the Dowager Queen
Of Inner and Outer Chaos—
Insists that I am Goldschmitt.

Coulette, I tell her, Coulette,
Fumbling my money-green passport.
I'm American, gentile,
And there's gas escaping somewhere!
She nods and mutters, Goldschmitt.

There is gas escaping somewhere,
And what does that evil stain
On the mattress signify?
Are you sure, are you damned sure,
This isn't the train to Deutschland?

Suddenly, unaccountably,
I sit down and write a letter
To the world, no! to the people
I love, no! to my family, yes!
The Family Goldschmitt.

AT THE HÔTEL DES SAINTS PÈRES

The Ginsbergs, *père et fils*,
Poètes extraordinaires,
Are in the courtyard below.
Their voices rustle like money.

Madame Dupon, who scorns me—
My French name, my lack of French—
Blesses their travelers cheques.
Her eyes are like ice cubes.

Sick with fever, needing a drink,
I read the Paris Trib:
The Red Sox are in first place,
And Rockwell the Nazi lies dead

In a parking lot in Dominion.
Sick with fever, sick for home,
For the black and the black-hearted,
I tip-toe to the window

To catch the English of the Ginsbergs.
It rises up and I *see* it!
There's a split infinitive,
And there's a four-letter word.

I must do something today.
I'd go to the grave of Baudelaire,
But I don't know where it is,
And I'm afraid to ask.

The pornographic bookshop—
It's caught itself on fire!

The Marquis, Frank Harris, and O—
The Travellers Companions are gone.

It's too late for words:
The pictures! Save the pictures!

We carry them out in our arms:
The Dark Lady, the Tattooed Man,

And Egypt, unbitten and bitten.
The fires have leaped from our eyes.

A silence is falling, and falls,
Out of which a man might speak,

But only the silence speaks,
And the ashes, the cold ashes.

ACID

Dostoevski would have loved
this two o'clock kitchen scene,
the shadows, the sixty watts!

Bobbie's had his sugar cube:
his two eyes are the sprung gates
of Paradise. I can read

nothing there, and the silence
is not the silence of stones
and feathers but the burnished

hum of the electric house.
Timeless in the midst of time—
that's what Bobbie wants to be.

Is it timeless where you are,
Bobbie? but he doesn't say,
or he says, *No, don't leave me,*

and I hear the dripping clock,
drop by burning drop, and sense,
ah! my own trip coming on,

though it be to a gaming
table, or a bitten tongue,
or another night like this.

He could not make up his mind:
It was like a bed rumpled
By a nightmare, the sheets, the blankets
Every which way. A new line
Appeared on the palm of each hand,

So he took long walks, imagining
Himself imaginary.
Yawn, snort, scratch—
He took up roses instead.
Or did roses take him up?

They put him on, anyway:
Mulch, thorns, aphids.
Finally, he took himself
Inside, where his shadow waited,
In a black chair, nodding.

SITUATION COMEDY

Grandma arrives first, of course,
In her chromium wheel chair,
Her hat on, her one leg tapping.
Mary Baker Eddy,
She tells us, has preserved her.

And Uncle Lee, prospector,
Who finds nothing, ever,
But a few rocks, rocks
That glow under black light,
Worthless and beautiful…

And then, my mother-in-law,
Who hated Adlai's shrewd eyes,
Who hates Kennedy's hair-do…
The crazy-quilt mantle
Of the Republic offends her.

Hangdog, my father-in-law
And I will wash dishes,
And plate by plate argue.
He's 1/32 Indian.
He wants to blow the world up.

Later, flatulent, stunned,
We'll all watch TV,
And hearing the laugh track—
Those tracks are thirty years old!—
We'll laugh as the dead laugh.

ON THE BALCONY

M.L.K., Jr.

The face in that window, blurred,
Broken, like an old moon…

My friends have assumed their shadows,
And look up at me, lingering…

The evening is hushed and ready,
Like a crowd I must speak to…

Something stirs in me,
Something I have forgotten…

It will come to me, and does,
And I am made public…

Dick is in the Blue Room,
With bourbon, bread, and cheese.
He cries the whole night long.

Pat comes to the door, hourly,
Clocking the dry sobs, clocking
The life of the Republic.

We feel sorry for them all,
Even Tricia, whose blonde hair
Fans out on a blue pillow:

Blue Dick, blue Pat, blue Tricia.
If the word *heart* were still used,
We would say that the heart

Of this importunate land
Was like an abandoned station
Somewhere beside broken tracks.

We will say, though, that the light
Falling on state documents,
That strong light, has a blue edge.

Bang! Bang! Bang!
And always in the head.
Click, and we're watching TV:
The Plane, the Widow, the Mass.
We drive with our lights on.

WALKING BACKWARDS

The horizon follows me.
The tall buildings lurch by.

I overtake someone,
Or someone turns and smiles.

We stop and make small talk:
—*Birth.* —*Love.* —*Death.*

They read the lines of boredom
In the rare book of my face.

They read between the lines
And turn away, hurt.

I leave them. I leave the squares
Of which I am an angle,

And the truths, the great truths,
At the ends of their chains, barking.

Truth is, we couldn't resist it.
Thank heaven for two-car garages.

It's at home there, a classic
Like a Rolls-Royce—but breathing:

Like having your very own
Diamond Match Company.

A conversation piece,
Except we don't talk about it.

Six nights in a row I've dreamt
Of a wall-eyed crossbowman,

And only moments ago
My wife came in, crown

Askew, arms akimbo,
The great tears rolling down,

To ask, *Are my ladies-in-waiting
Still waiting?* and ran to her room.

Lying beside this poem,
It cares no more for it
Than the dead care for black borders.

The runt of a litter of two,
It has never been housebroken,
Retrieves only the small evils:

The drink, the smoke, the pill.
Even in the act of love,
It wanders away, bored.

A pure anarchist, it salutes
Not even the black flag.
Those long naps—what do they mean?

A grooming of itself for death,
The lily thereof? I hope not.
I should miss, somehow, its maundering.

DOORS

The two-sided nature of doors
Is disturbing to lovers.

They would have them have
One side only as walls have.

We can forgive the lovers—
And haven't we always?—

Their being so unhinged
By hints of duplicity.

Trust, rather, the pensioners,
Who know that doors yawn

As friends do at daybreak,
And that they close like wings.

For the newborn
The Americas

For the working stiff
A natural harbor

For the trueloves
The open seas

For memory
A graveyard

The first cry, the last word
Apertures

I read in a strange book,
While the sunlight moves on my back
And the dog at my foot stretches:

No word is ever lost,
For all sound circles the earth,
Like a noose or a wristwatch.

The sun moves off. The dog sleeps.
I close the book, and the sound
Of the book closing rises,

A thread of hemp, a small jewel,
Among the quotations, flying,
Famous and infamous.

I think of your cry of pain,
Of myself, once, reciting,
Amo, amas, amat.

ON ACCOUNT

The tax-man would be around,
Late at night, subpoena in hand,

If what you are really worth
Would lend itself to numbers,

To columns, red ink, black ink…
I am writing this poem, you know,

In my check book, in black ink.
You can cash it, if you like.

I must be in your next poem,
She says, smiling, her fingers
Autographing my knee.

Flashback, and I am there,
Fugitive, in a grey garden,
Croaking, *Here I am, here I am,*

The tall prince, terribly hidden
Under a crown of warts;
And they came, the flaxen, the raven,

In their long gowns, clinging.
They came kissing my green skin,
But their kisses would not take.

Unhand me, madam, I have—
More electric than Kiss,
As promising as Change—

All that this frog needs:
Tobacco, alcohol, ink,
And the hue of metaphor crying.

TODAY I BEGIN MY FIRST NOVEL

On my porch, the characters gather,
Or wander the garden, gathering
The sick rose, the shattered daisy.

Neglect, Neglect, they cry out,
Meaning Knock, meaning Begin,
The girl who is the sick rose,

The crone like a grey flag,
My dead father coming toward me—
Stop, I say, meaning Start,

And I start looking up plots:
*A, who must eat his words,
And is trapped in the city of X,*

*Befriends the mute A-2,
An Unknown, who eats the berries
Of a strange plant and goes mad,*

*While B, before her mirror,
Discovers she has spent the night
As she ought not to have done—*

Ridiculous, the crone cries.
Child, my father shouts,
Carrying the rose in his arms

As if she were my mother.
The garden is filling with snow.
Tomorrow I begin the sequel.

You might have worn bandages,
Sir, like in the old story.

After all, you were a wound,
Or at best, the breath of Absence.

One of us said, once, that you stood
On the dark side of Mother.

I think now that you stood
Behind us, like the sun,

Fathering our shadows toward her.
You have become the music

You practiced hours and hours
Elsewhere in that strange house,

The difficult passage I hear
Suddenly in context.

NINE

You have been to see *Frankenstein*
And you can't sleep, or won't.

Your father is running bathwater.
A radio plays somewhere.

If you cried out, Mother
Would come, shushing, calming,

Her eyes haunted and haunting.
You drift in the tall darkness.

If you were to dream yourself
Elsewhere, later, older,

Remembering this moment,
Would you cry out? And why?

THE POET AT ELEVEN

for the Brown Bomber

All those white hopes on their backs.
In the backyard, twilit,
My father's '25 Chandler
With the mohair seats
And the little flower vases…

I sat there, glasses fogged,
Turning the strange words over.
Madison Square Garden.
Madison Square Garden.
All those fights among the roses!

Romero in dark glasses,
Cat-like on the main street...

Past the pool hall, the Lodge.
What was his friend's name?

It will come to me later.
Saturday nights at the Lensic:

Barbara Stanwyck. Afterwards,
We would hear the drunks singing,

And watch the millers circling.
We knew we were going to die;

Our blood, bittersweet, running.
We didn't, or I didn't. His name...

What was his name? What was mine?
1943.

ON MANGE L'ORANGE ET JETTE L'ÉCORCE

for Henri Déricourt, double agent

1.

I had come to think of you
As a fiction, like Zero,
Infinity, or Ulysses.

Now, you confound me, dying,
As fictions never do.
Zero says, *Hello, Henri.*

Infinity says, *Goodbye.*
Ulysses, that salt shadow?
No comment, and turns away.

2.

It is the Forties, and you sit
Outdoors at the Brasserie Lipp.
The wind ruffles the pages

Of your book. Racine? No!
No, it would be Baudelaire,
And the wind, ruffling so,

On a certain dogeared page
Shall find certain words
Underscored, *n'est-ce pas?*

3.

In Auschwitz, in Belsen, in Dachau,
It is the Forties, also,
And the wind, the same wind,

A branch of the same wind,
Ruffles the funny beards
Of the Family Goldschmitt,

And the hair, the long dark hair
Of the women standing there,
Naked, with their secret beards.

So long a line, the guards say,
Dreaming of gold teeth,
And the small rain down doth rain.

4.

A raindrop or two fall
On the never-to-be-ciphered page.
You snap the *Flowers* shut,

Get up, and disappear
Among the black umbrellas
Opening everywhere.

ON THE HORIZON

for John Trainor

It is just what he had imagined,
A blue-chalk line
Such as girls use, summers,
For hop-scotch.

He crosses over it,
The left slipper first,
For luck, and then

The right forever.

If he were to look back—
But he won't,
He's beyond that—

He would see, the light being right,
Everything
As it always intended itself.

Is the cease-fire over, Venus?
Spare me! Spare me! I beg you to remember
I am not what I once was
When under the gentle thumb of Cynara. Forbear,

Cruel mother of the Cupids,
To put the screws to one now pushing fifty,
Now cold to your hot breath.
Go whither the young are praying up a storm;

On purple swansdown go,
Revel in the house of Paulus Maximus,
And seek what you must seek,
That someone who would burn most hard, most gem-like.

Noble and handsome both,
The champion of the divorcée and the widow,
A youth of a hundred skills,
He shall bear your standards into the hinterlands;

And when some giver of gifts,
Some lavish rival, fails, Paulus, laughing,
Will set you up in marble
Under a citrus roof near the Alban Lake.

There you will breathe only
The best of incense, and there be charmed by a concert
Featuring the lyre,
The Berecynthian flute and the reedpipe, too.

There a boy and a girl will dance
In your honor twice a day, day in, day out,
The dance of the Salian,
And shake the earth three times with a bare foot.

Nothing—nor girl, nor boy,
The credulous hope of being loved by either,
Nor grape, the trials thereof,
Nor flowers fresh upon my brow—delights me.

Nothing. Then why, Lygurinus,
Does a tear now and then trickle down my gray cheek?
Why does my eloquent tongue
Fall with an unbecoming silence among these words?

Now, in the dream of night,
I hold you captive; now I pursue you in flight
Over the grasses of the Campus
Martius, O hard-hearted, through the whirling waters.

Being French, being 19th century, we know about boredom.
It is a glove, and having invented sex,
We know that the sex of the glove does not matter:

A glove, a simple glove, over the angry knuckles taut,
Over the long fingers twitching, over the three
Mad stars of the palm sweating, over the Devil's Workshop;

And where the glove opens like a wound, a bell, a mouth,
The pulse tongues out the one word *All*,
Which is to say *Absolute*, which is to say

Everything in our grasp, and we grasp the shoulder
Of a chair like the chair we knelt on, bare-kneed children
Saying our Aves, and the chair heard us out,

O Mother of π and radii and the irregular verb,
Of the Spitwad Wars and the elephants of Hannibal,
Of Doctor and Nurse, two times, in the cloakroom—

O Mother, hear us now in the hour of our knees!
All that was childwood, and the typographical error
Is not, repeat not, to be corrected; it is all

That remains of our innocence. We are grown-up now,
Which is to say *metaphysical*, which is to say *bored*.
On these long 19th century evenings, we walk the Boulevard,

Asking ourselves, What of the explosion in the desert,
The one no one witnessed? Was there sound there?
Or only the silence of Him in His long sleep?

And the chair? Does it become invisible even to itself?
Or does it dance the grave, stiff-legged Dance of the Chairs,
Our absence all around it like a strange music?

Or does it stand, faithful, in the desert of the mind,
And shall we welcome it, happily, reverently,
As wisemen an oasis, as children a mirage?

Today, they are the subjects of a king,
And they must cheer his passage through the town
This coronation morning, cheer his taking
Purple and ermine, the sceptre and the crown.

They have, they will again, take after take,
But now the star, his agent at his sleeve,
Has disappeared. Their thoughts come back to them,
Like shadows, and they rest from make-believe.

Duchess and chimney sweep are Blossom and Hank.
A light is asked for, and a light is given.
Gossip is music played upon the breath
By wicked tongues, and anecdote is heaven.

Simply human is what their costumes smell of;
Simply human is what their faces say.
They make the lobby and the street look real.
Practicing every day for Judgment Day,

They draw the circle that becomes a crown;
They draw bathwater on a bended knee,
And curtains on the night, and they draw blood.
They are the after that comes After Me.

AT THE GRAVE OF THE FOURTH MAN

for Jean Maloney

You know the scene: the standard black umbrella
Against the public rain, and in the fist
A handkerchief in memory of the tear
That would not well, and is not really missed.

What had been tucked into the *TLS*
The blindman left beside the sloe-eyed beauty
Languishing at the bar? And who was the hunchback
Who idled while his poodle did its duty?

Characters, characters all, like aces, like faces
On playing cards, and the cards, of course, were marked.
What was it Noah whispered in each ear
As one by one the agents disembarked?

To live a double life? Or just keep dry?
That would be telling, and they refuse to tell,
Or sell, their secrets to the likes of us,
The ordinary folk of Lesser Hell.

After they lived happily ever after,
The sky was perfect, being without cloud,
Without a trace of any sort of weather.

Greenwich did not exist. One was not struck,
Ever, and the mouse did not run up the clock;
And the unicorn's head was always in someone's lap.

If he had been moved to speech, he would have gone
Beyond speech into song, into nonsense, into scat,
O nonny, nonny, O hey nonny, O!

And what would you guess? That she smiled? Well, of course.
It was the one expression vouchsafed her.
It was a perfectly accurate, mindless smile.

In our world, where even the rose must cast a shadow,
Moonlit Greenwich would mill their scented hours;
Et in Arcadia Ego, would marvel the mouse;

And they would dream of others, and meet others, and weep.

TEA DANCE AT THE NAUTILUS HOTEL (1925)

On a painting by Donald Justice

The blue-haired lady with the ebony cane,
Down to the right out of sight, undergoes gold,
As if Midas himself had written the Book of Ayres,
As if, as if...
          Meanwhile, all grace, pure swan,
The dancers wend their way among the palms,
In pastel frocks, in silk suits impeccably tailored,
Their bow ties like butterflies, their patents gleaming.
What is this ditty called? they ask each other,
And whisper Rabbit and Bear, and whisper Hyena.

THE SILENT Y

for Ruth Sandys

X has been discarded; Z we will not get to.
We are left with the second unknown. In your case,
The sweet mute, the dear dumb, the silent Y.

It passes in the font for one more humdrum
Hardworking first cousin to O, a half-brother of X,
The love child of the question mark.

But taken up, given the freedom of the mouth,
Its lead becomes gold, and it comes before the lover's moan;
It follows on the heel of the dead man's sigh.

The color of it? The color of silence, Ruth?
Frederick who lived his days in a north light,
His nights with a darkness in the darkness—

Frederick answered that above his signature.
You are your great-grandfather's great daughter.
You are the silence that shall be heard from.

Wyatt takes up his quill. Henry has spoken.
Newfangleness goes gadding hereabout.
Farewell is honed, and every promise broken.

A scullion dreams he let the fire die out,
And has, and will be thrashed with a mule's tether.
In his small dream, there is no room for doubt.

In the King's mews, his favorite moults a feather.
Catherine weeps, as Henry goes to see
Anne under ermine in the altogether.

It is late March of 1533.

NEWFANGLENESS

What can be said? An oriel explodes.
A staircase, like a spilled accordion,
Drops to its knees and groans.
Newel and banister part.
The wrecking ball doth murder the bedroom cupid.

The young are writing what they call free verse.
Their fingers have forgotten how to count,
Those delicate long fingers.
No Anne Boleyn now would sigh,
Struck by the cunning of her Wyatt's measure.

Old rooms, old tunes, old loves—all of them gone.
The watch is relentless, but its chime is sweet.
Take up the minus sign—
Go, run with the Abyss:
You lose what you must love, yet you must love.

The blonde mane, the impossible blue of the eyes,
The black velvet jacket, the four gold frogs,
The white lace at the throat, at the white wrist,

And the blue vein, that small hammer at the wrist,
Like squaring the circle, or a grooming of griffins, or a black rose,
And the verdict in, kudos to the jury, the jury gone home,

And the judge shucking his black robe in his possible chamber,
And the verdict is guilty, and the sentence forever,
Forever the black rose, the blue eyes, the blonde mane…

What was your motive? I don't remember. I refuse to remember.
And the weapon? Guilty. And the weapon? Yes.
And the blue hammer, yes, impossible, mine, and forever.

REMEMBRANCE OF THINGS FUTURE

I.

You arrive in a new town.
Your suitcase yawns. Your troubles
Unpack themselves and dress up.
A night on the town! Poor town.

The wallpaper reminds you
Of a story or poem
You started once in a room
Much like this room, this poem.

You will dial Room Service
And order a fifth of gin.
You will drink an inch of it,
Clear as cellophane, and laugh,

Having heard in the next room
The shuffle of playing cards.
You will knock. You will sit in.
You will fill your inside straights.

II.

You are the tall dark stranger, and his ghost.
You will forgive. You will forget. Almost.

III.

You will apologize & apologize & apologize.
You are Henry James.
You are Japanese.

Tennessee is a string on your finger.
Tennessee is you with your pants down,
And you own up to it.

Tennessee is a train coming in,
And you lost in the steam of it,
And the gray mail-bags falling.

You will come, later, to the edge.
You will hone it. You will cut yourself.
You will apologize.

IV.

If the violin attacks, if the mirror changes
its spots, are the leopards to be left untuned?

You lay broad waking, the two of you, in a
motel in Phoenix. You will not be that happy again,
ever.

V.

There are those who dream of keys.
There are those who dream of locks.

You dream of neither. You are the key;
You are the lock. There is no turning.

You are like a good novelist.
Your characters never open doors,

Never close them. And when they speak,
They say *thou*, they say *thee*.

VI.

If your mother should live again in a dream,
and turn and look at you, as she did so often,
and should she, yes, whisper, *Shipwreck*, you must
answer, *Cage*.

VII.

This is the day you have been waiting for.
The morning should be set aside for thought:
Hunker down naked under such a hat
As one sees disappearing around corners,
A broad black hat. Pretending to some boredom,
But only some, conjure the absolute.
It will seem under that brim that you get
Moment by moment more and more immortal.

The grand confusions! Have you got them straight?
Never mind. Evening is another story:
You, robed in shadow, all garlanded by light,
A prince grown weary of posing for his portrait—

You nod and dream, and dream yourself complete,
This evening of the day you waited for.

VIII.

Of your absence newly acquired,
The O of astonishment, the Q of death,

Nothing, they will say nothing.
They will say, The vineyard of his palm,

And on the shelf, gleaming, the brims
That leaned into and tasted his mouth.

All has been translated into amber.
All has been poured into your cups.

And the tongue cried more, more.
And the tongue cried never enough.

IX.

The bear, the broom, the butterfly…

The bear is for misfortune.
It shambles toward you, ten feet tall,
For that is the exact height,
Always, of misfortune. Always.

New prospects ahead, the broom says,
Or would say, if brooms spoke,

But all the broom does is go shush, shush,
Sweeping the bear away, the bear away.

The butterfly says, *Much happiness,*
Says, *Unexpected pleasure,*
All in the tongue of the butterfly
Which is the tongue of the future.

2. THE SINGLE LIFE

Being a bachelor's not so hot.
I find I sleep on the wet spot.

3.

Caesar's seizures were all the same.
He saw, she conquered, and they came.

4. THE WHOLE STORY

In Camelot, King Arthur came a lot,
With two queens, Guinevere and Lancelot.

7. THE COLLECTED POEMS OF WHAT'S HIS FACE

Sixteen thousand lines, give or take sixteen—
And no two lines that you can read between.

8.

Everything here is Spanish but the fly.
My name, Señor, she is Roberto Bly.

12.

I understand your tongue. I get the message.
You are a good book open to the best passage.

13.

Everything still is as it was arranged:
Bird song, and a green shadow on the sill;
The lilac in its silver vase. Still. Still,
It must be autumn, for your eyes have changed.

15.

When memory takes over from desire,
You need a drink, and in the hearth, a fire.

16.

A one-eyed cat named Hathaway on my lap,
A fire in the fireplace, and Schubert's 5th
All silvery somewhere on a radio
I barely hear, but hear—this is, I think,
As close as I may come to happiness.

NIGHT THOUGHTS

in memory of David Kubal

Your kind of night, David, your kind of night.
The dog would eye you as you closed your book;
Such a long chapter, such a time it took
The great leaps! The high cries! The leash like a line drive!
The two of you would rove the perfumed street,
Pillar to post, and terribly alive.

Your kind of night, nothing more, nothing less;
A single lighted window, the shade drawn,
Your shadow enormous on the silver lawn,
The busy mockingbird, his rapturous fit,
The cricket keeping time, the loneliness
Of the man in the moon—and the man under it.

The word *elsewhere* was always on your lips,
A password to some secret, inner place
Where Wisdom smiled in Beautie's looking-glass
And Pleasure was at home to dearest Honour.
(The dog-eared pages mourn your fingertips,
And vehicle whispers, *Yet once more*, to tenor.)

Now you are elsewhere, *elsewhere* comes to this,
The thoughtless body, like a windblown rose,
Is gathered up and ushered toward repose.
To have to know this is our true condition,
The Horn of Nothing, the classical abyss,
The only cry a cry of recognition.

The priest wore purple; now the night does, too.
A dog barks, and another, and another.
There are a hundred words for the word *brother*.
We use them when we love, when we are sick,
And in our dreams when we are somehow you.
What are we if not wholly catholic?

They knew the conjugations of the flesh;
I knew the day's lesson.
A noun is the name of a person, place, or thing.

I did the possible:
I memorized their names, smiled my smile,
And taught, small miracle,

One girl, Carolyn Bywater, to tell time,
And tell it she did, by God!
Each minute past became a fallen sparrow.

One June day a bell rang.
They left. They went out into their lives, and left
The squeak in the chalk forever.

That was a thousand thousand sparrows ago.
They are like old bluebooks now—
Telling, untold, indecipherable.

AT THE GRAVEYARD

for Minnie Patterson (1873-1971)

We have come a little early. Minutes away in the small town
You painted your pictures of, where you wrote your cheerful verse,
They are turning the screws of a gray coffin. Your coffin.

We wander among the headstones, killing time, saying what we have said
All day, *What a beautiful day*, meaning the high clouds, the high wind,
The blue there is no name for, except sky, except beautiful.

We have come to the stones of the far side, the stones of the last century.
There are so many children here, and here is a man born in Damascus—
A Country Doctor for 40 Years to Our County—

And his wife—Clara, A Descendant of Jonathan Edwards.
The day is beautiful, the sky is blue, the clouds are clouds
You cannot read anything into. They are simply clouds.

The hearse comes down the highway, and turns, and stops.
We make our way toward you, past the Lieutenant of Cavalry,
The Native of Iowa, Our Beloved Father, His Sweet Child.

CORRESPONDENCE

The letter lies unanswered, thus free of lies.
The light all day has travelled the crowded pages,
Shifting the shadows, changing the hue of ink.
The truths, if truths there are, are stationary.

Now night comes on, from your time zone to mine.
The moon is tentative, not wholly herself,
And the owl bells, and the owl's mate bells back,
A dialogue of sorts, question and answer,

The answer being but the question asked.
East of your sleep, deep in the zodiac,
Tomorrow is already chronicled.
Oh, I shall write you what you want to hear.

There are some questions one should know by heart.
A world without them must be shadowless.
Who was it said, Come let us kiss and part?

The one who asked, Why is this apple tart?
And dreamed the serpent was the letter S?
There are some questions one should know by heart.

It was the thorn that plotted to outsmart
The cunning of the rose with such success.
Who was it said, Come let us kiss and part?

There are interiors none may map or chart:
In your voice, crying, was a wilderness.
There are some questions one should know by heart.

Your ape and echo from the bitter start,
This mirror mourns your image's caress.
Who was it said, Come let us kiss and part?

We had too little craft and too much art.
We thought two noes would make a perfect yes.
There are some questions one should know by heart.
Who was it said, Come let us kiss and part?

A spare tire some boy spanked all summer long,
Its bald spot showing, leans
A sleepy head against a broken wall.

The wall leans back and whispers,
Truth is not beauty, beauty is not truth,
As is the wont of walls,

Especially if broken. The wall reads,
Paco, Shorty, Grunt,
The names the poets took before they left.

That soughing at the sill—
Is it a requiem for the fisted spider,
His harvest a tall crown

Of iridescent ruins, of tiny shipwrecks:
The nature of things fragile
Made manifest?

Yes, and the boy made a man.

PETITION

Lord of the Tenth Life,
Welcome my Jerome,
A fierce, gold tabby.
Make him feel at home.

He loves bird and mouse.
He loves a man's lap,
And in winter light,
Paws tucked in, a nap.

THE GARDEN

I do the crossword in my backyard garden.
The clue is *Age*. Rags, my tattered companion,
Barks at a mockingbird. The bird barks back,
A rogue, in Rags's fabulous opinion.

Age is a lifetime, a chinoiserie
Of aches and pains, is being slightly vague,
The wit of the staircase while falling down,
Wisdom, though wisdom may be just fatigue.

The great world rages at the garden gate,
Crying my childhood name with siren voices,
Pressing for one more go at plenitude.
Too late, too late, for I have cut my losses.

To change as music changes, note by note,
Recovering the theme, and come to closure—
Now that would be an unofficial joy,
A private substitute for the world's pleasure.

One has illusions even about that.
The glories nod. A hummingbird whirrs by,
Towing the purple evening in its wake.
Venus regards the garden with a clear eye.

LATE LOVE, A COMIC OPERA

We'll have no litany of our aches and pains,
As some rehearse, and always with tremulous sighs,
As if competing for some grand last prize.
O clap of thunder, O funereal rains!
Nor envy the young, under their counterpanes,
The trying of each other on for size.
Everything fits! they cry, in rapt surprise—
As bridles fit, headstall, bit, and reins.

The overture is over. The curtain rises.
Two maids in working black, with fluting voices,
Speak of a couple of a certain age.
There has been gossip… if left to their own devices…
It isn't for the likes of us to judge!
They giggle and arrange the perfect roses.

Blue is the color of my true love's hair,
     And blue her eyes, ·
    Her almost lavender eyes.
  The young push past her in the aisle?
And shake their thoughtless heads? She mustn't care.
    The old have their own style.

I offer myself here as one example.
     These azure mornings
    I wonder how many mornings
  The almanac holds for me still.
There's nothing in all this world so pure, so simple,
    So unalterable.

What of the pensioners in Paradise?
     And do they miss
    The things that I would miss?
  The telephone with its wrong number,
The flyers for Occupant, the midnight mouse,
    And Rags pretending to slumber?

I am content. I seldom say *If only*,
     For what is past
    Redemption *is* the past,
  An out-of-date book about love
That you might turn to when you think you're lonely
    Or blue, the color of…

Elsewhere in Rutherford, thanks to his hands,
Mother and child have entered the new world,
Separate now, save for the one shadow.

Medicine henceforth will be all mother—
A laxative, a mustard plaster, a kiss.
The boy will grow, grow hair, and grow beyond her.

And there will be a war, and he will go.
The mother will send pictures of herself,
Taken too late to capture what she was.

Chest full of ribbons, a condom in his boot,
He will straddle a stool at an Owl Drug, and gaze
At a red-headed girl in a tight skirt.

The good and naked doctor, emptied now
Of those anatomies, more gray than Gray,
Will sleep for a few hours, his mouth open.

UNCOLLECTED POEMS

on a Penitente figure-in-the-round

St. Francis has a face to frighten birds;
His eyes like olive pits, his nose half gone.
This crumbling doll—it seems a skeleton,
So narrow is the waist the rough rope girds.

Who puts in wood what no one puts in words?
No wonder our canary tries to shun
This image. Francis smiled his orison,
Charming the singing flocks and lowing herds.

Brother Wolf, Sister Lark, who masquerades
In Friar's habit? Why does he prolong
His vigil, questioning our earthly trades?

Silent as stone, louder than a gong,
His passion, darkening the room, persuades
The caged canary to abandon song.

A law unto themselves, the Keystone Cops
Deserve our praise. It is no simple task,
The thoughtful wearing of the comic mask;
Their standards higher than the chimney tops,
They study that profound extravagance
One finds in anger, love, or a wine cask;
Their hearts must answer what their minds may ask:
True comedy requires the tragic sense.

The bastard sons of Pan, they sometimes rage
With too much whiskey or with broken minds,
Reduced to straight men on the runway boards,
Their genius thwarted by the bumps and grinds,
Or worse, they conjure up a floodlit stage,
And scream their ad libs in the loony wards.

Cry figs, my love, on totem and taboo
And end this argument, for we agree
That in the dark the darkness takes its due,

For we agree on what we always knew,
The heart moves quicker than the eye can see.
Cry figs, my love, on totem and taboo

And sigh, for hearts, like lions in a zoo,
Dream of a country where the wild are free,
Where in the dark the darkness takes its due.

Copy the vine which wandering as it grew
Reached heaven in the branches of a tree.
Cry figs, my love, on totem and taboo.

At last, the sun is fading—that's our cue!
This bed's our stage, those stars our gallery.
When in the dark the darkness takes its due

And I, beloved, tremble next to you,
Laugh in my ear and whisper this to me:
Cry figs, my love, on totem and taboo…
Now, in the dark, the darkness takes its due.

[THE SALT PACIFIC BEATS AT MALIBU]

The salt Pacific beats at Malibu;
We think we hear it even from the Strip.
The wine is native, of an amber hue—
What spirit hovers at the brimming lip?

Drink up! A long apprenticeship is ended.
Bid welcome to whatever ghosts may come,
And let no man or phantom be offended,
For now, this night, the homeless are at home.

The fragrant shore, the vineyards in the sand—
We come between the desert and the sea,
Exiles returning to our native land,
Accepting now what we are bound to be.

The pans and dishes are unpacked,
The books are heavy on the shelves,
The bed is waiting like a prize
With which you will reward yourselves.

You have forgotten even now
The house where yesterday you lived;
Already you become the place
Where you this moving day arrived.

We are the creaking door and step,
The faucet that will always drip
—We are the presences that hold
All ruin in receivership.

Be without fear, for we are gentle,
The ghosts of all the tenants past,
The image you have just become,
An image that will always last,

Of history the milling dust
The future cannot help but breathe,
The sum of all your days and nights,
The legacy your lives bequeath.

Jack Donne and Raymond Chandler, like shattered pigeons, fall,
All thud and blunder, quintessential California.

A name like Richter gives a signature to fear,
And palm tree rats now hearken to the lisp of God.

The swimming pools of Eden suddenly are empty.
Bertolt Brecht's spectacles lie splintered on the floor,

For all the world is made of glass and makes to break,
And shines like stars without a heaven, and makes to cut.

Alas, O children of paradise, it comes to this:
This bed thy centre was, that is a midnight mouth.

ACKNOWLEDGEMENTS

We extend our gratitude to William Patrick O'Reilly for permission to publish his uncle's poems and for all the help he has given us, and to Jacqueline Coulette for her blessing and support. Erik Pedersen, whose passion for Coulette's work and research into his life led to the publication of an important profile in *The Orange County Register* in March 2023, provided crucial assistance. Dana Gioia, who has done more than anyone to preserve the literary legacy of Los Angeles, offered invaluable advice and constant encouragement. Robert Erickson was kind enough to publish a version of our introduction as an essay in *The New Criterion*, a journal where a number of Coulette's finest late poems appeared in the 1980s. Last but certainly not least, we are deeply grateful to the team at Carcanet—Michael Schmidt, Andrew Latimer, and Alan Brenik—for their faith in this project.

Either in time or manner, the poems of the first section are early. The order of the other sections is simply chronological.

The penultimate line of "The Black Angel" is from a poem by LBG-30.

One-third of "The Sickness of Friends" is the work of Philip Levine.

"The War of the Secret Agents" is based on Jean Overton Fuller's remarkable *Double Webs*.

The penultimate line of the penultimate stanza of "The Blue-Eyed Precinct Worker" is from a mystery by Ross Macdonald.